Index

Reach the Caffarella Valley

Entrance from Largo Pietro Tacchi Venturi

From **Piazza San Giovanni**: Take the 87 bus line towards Largo Colli Albani and get off at Menghini-Crivellucci stop. Walk for about 150 meters.

From **the Colosseum**: go to bus stop Labicana-Colosseum and take the 87 line towards Largo Colli Albani and get off at Menghini-Crivellucci stop. Walk for 150 meters.

From **Termini Station**: take the metro line A direction Anagnina and get off at Colli Albani. Walk for 450 meters.

From **Tuscolana Station**: go to Piazza Ragusa stop and take bus line 665 towards of Piazza San Giovanni in Laterano. Get off at Fortifiocca-Baronio stop and take bus line 87 towards Largo Colli Albani and get off at Menghini-Crivellucci stop. Walk for 150 meters.

From **Tiburtina station**: go to the Tiburtina station and take the metro line B direction Laurentina. Take metro line A direction Anagnina and get off at Colli Albani. Walk for 450 meters.

Entrance from Via Appia Pignatelli

From **Piazza San Giovanni**: go to stop Piazza San Giovanni in Laterano. Take bus line 714 (towards Palazzo dello Sport) for 2 stops or bus line 792 (towards Eur). Get off at Terme di Caracalla. Go to stop Porta San Sebastiano / Numa Pompilio. Take bus line 118 (towards Appia/Villa dei Quintili) for 9 stops. Get off at stop Appia Pignatelli/S. Urbano.

From **Piazza del Colosseo**: go to stop Celio/Vibenna. Take bus line 118 (towards Appia/Villa dei Quintili) for 13 stops. Get off at stop Appia Pignatelli/S. Urbano.

From **Stazione Termini**: go to stop Termini. Take bus line 714 (towards Palazzo dello Sport) for 7 stops. Get off at stop Terme di Caracalla. Porta San Sebastiano / Numa Pompilio. Take bus line 118 (towards Appia/Villa dei Quintili) for 9 stops. Get off at stop Appia Pignatelli/S. Urbano.

From **Stazione Tuscolana**: go to the stop Ragusa. Take bus line 85 (towards Termini) for 11 stops. Get off at the Fori Imperiali. Take bus line 118 (towards Appia / Villa dei Quintili) for 15 stops. Get off at stop Appia Pignatelli/S. Urbano.

From **Stazione Tiburtina**: go to stop Stazione Tiburtina. Take the Metro line B (towards Laurentina) for 7 stops. Get off at Circo Massimo. Go to stop Terme di Caracalla/Porta Capena. Take bus line 118 (towards Appia) for 11 stops. Get off at Appia Pignatelli/S. Urbano.

From **Stazione Ostiense**: go to stop Ostiense/Matteucci. Take bus line 716 (towards Teatro Marcello) for 7 stops. Get off at the stop Petroselli. Take bus line 118 (towards Appia / Villa dei Quintili) for 18 stops. Get off at stop Appia Pignatelli/S. Urbano.

From **Piazza Del Popolo**: go to stop Maria Adelaide. Take the bus line 628 (towards Baronio) for 13 stops. Get off at Terme di Caracalla/Valle Camene. Take bus line 118 (towards Appia/Villa dei Quintili) for 10 stops. Get off at stop Appia Pignatelli/S. Urbano.

Entrance from Via Macedonia

From **Piazza del Popolo:** go to stop Maria Adelaide. Take bus line 628 (towards Baronio) for 20 stops. Get off at the stop Gregorovius. Walk for 150 meters.

From **Piazza San Giovanni:** go to stop Porta San Giovanni. Take bus line 665 for 9 stops. Get off at the stop Gregorovius. Walk for 150 meters

From **Piazza del Colosseo**: go to stop Celio/Vibenna. Take bus line 118 (Appia/ Villa Quintili) for 2 stops. Get off at Terme di Caracalla/Porta Capena. Take bus line 628 (Baronio) for 8 stops. Get off at the stop Gregorovius. Walk for 150 meters

From **Stazione Termini**: go to stop Termini. Take the Metro line A (towards Anagnina) for 5 stops. Get off at Ponte Lungo. Go to the stop Gela. Take bus line 665 (towards Piazza San Giovanni in Laterano) for 7 stops. Get off at the stop Macedonia. Walk for 50 meters

From **Stazione Tiburtina**. Go to Stazione Tiburtina. Take the line FL1 (towards Fiumicino) to 1 stops. Get off at the Stazione Tuscolana. Go to stop Monselice/ Stazione Tuscolana. Take bus line 665 (towards Piazza San Giovanni in Laterano) for 8 stops. Get off at the stop Macedonia. Walk for 50 meters

From **Stazione Ostiense**: go to stop Ostiense/Matteucci. Take bus line 716 (towards eatro Marcello) for 7 stops. Get off at the stop Petroselli. Take bus line 628 (Baronio) for 12 stops. Get off at the stop Gregorovius. Walk for 150 meters.

Framework of the maps union

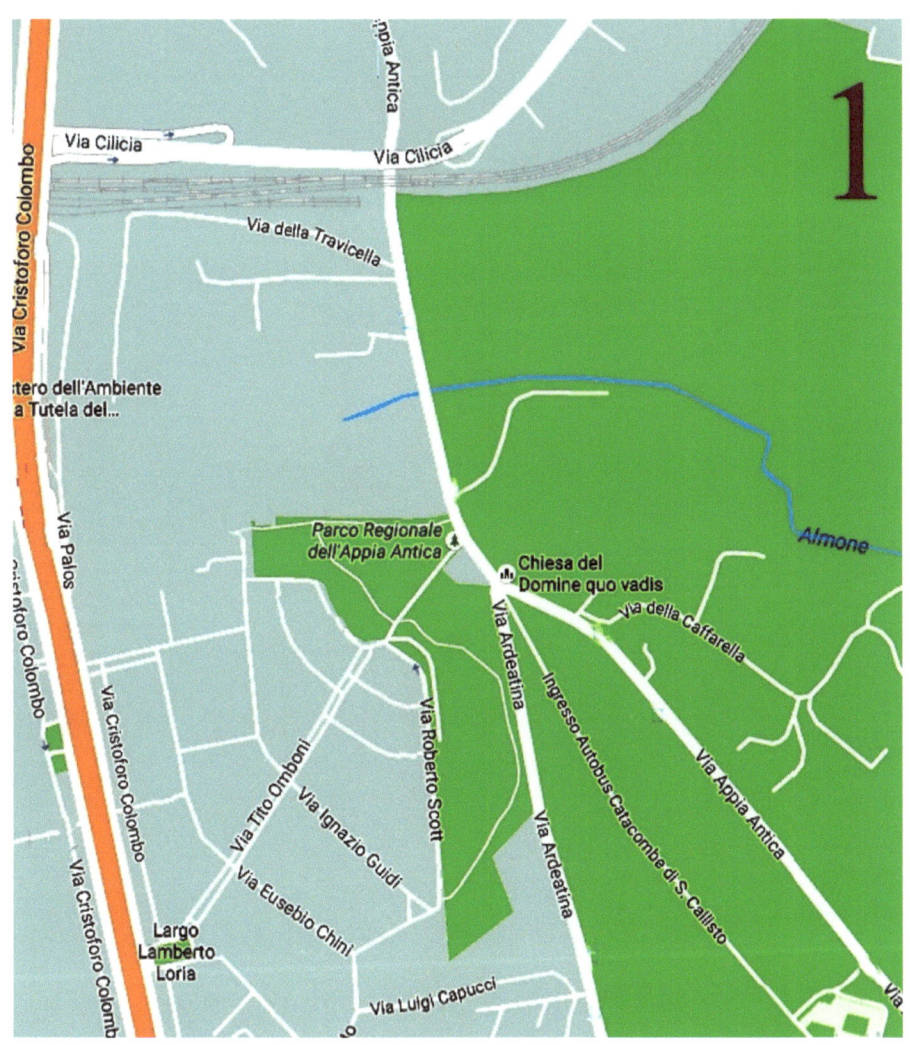

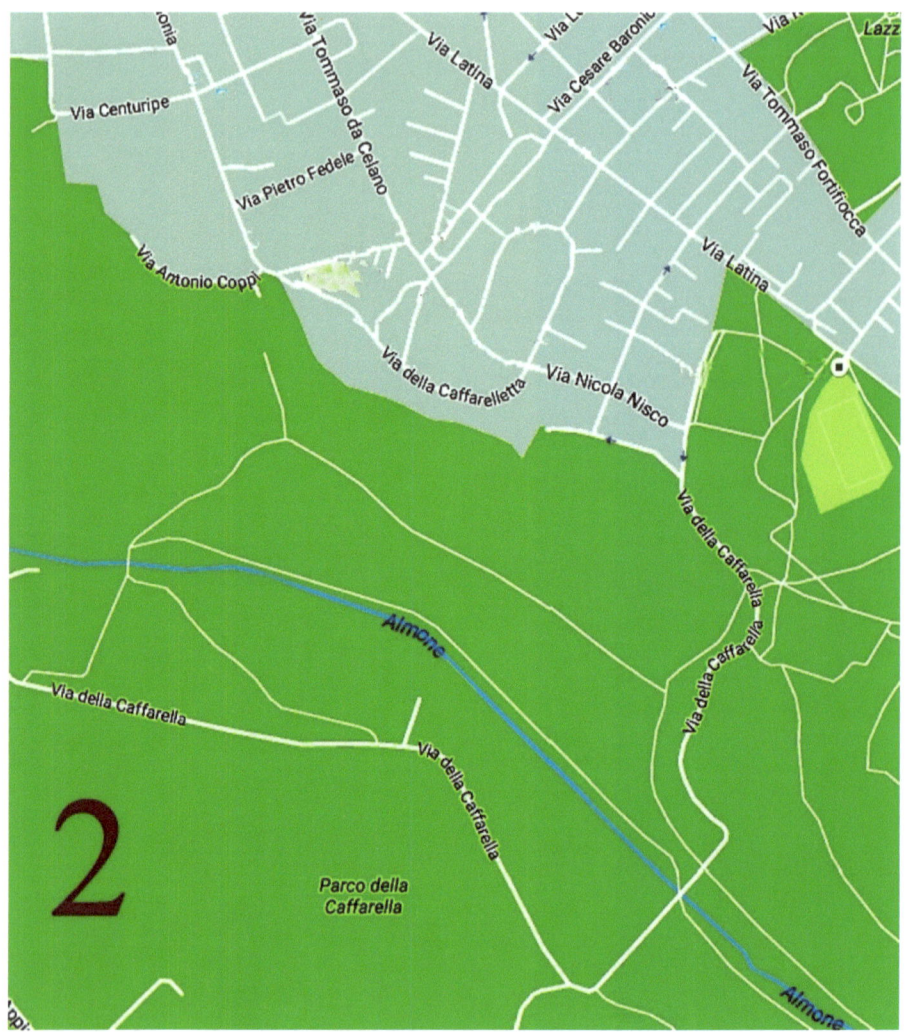

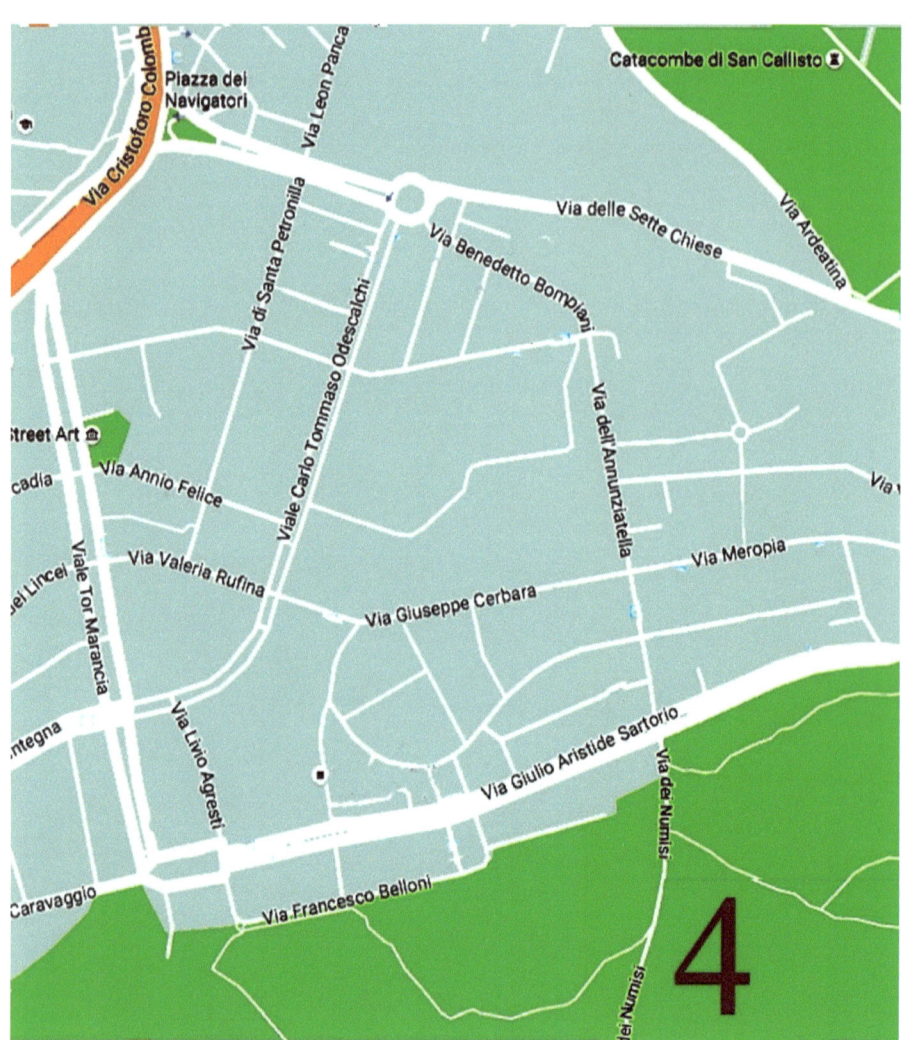

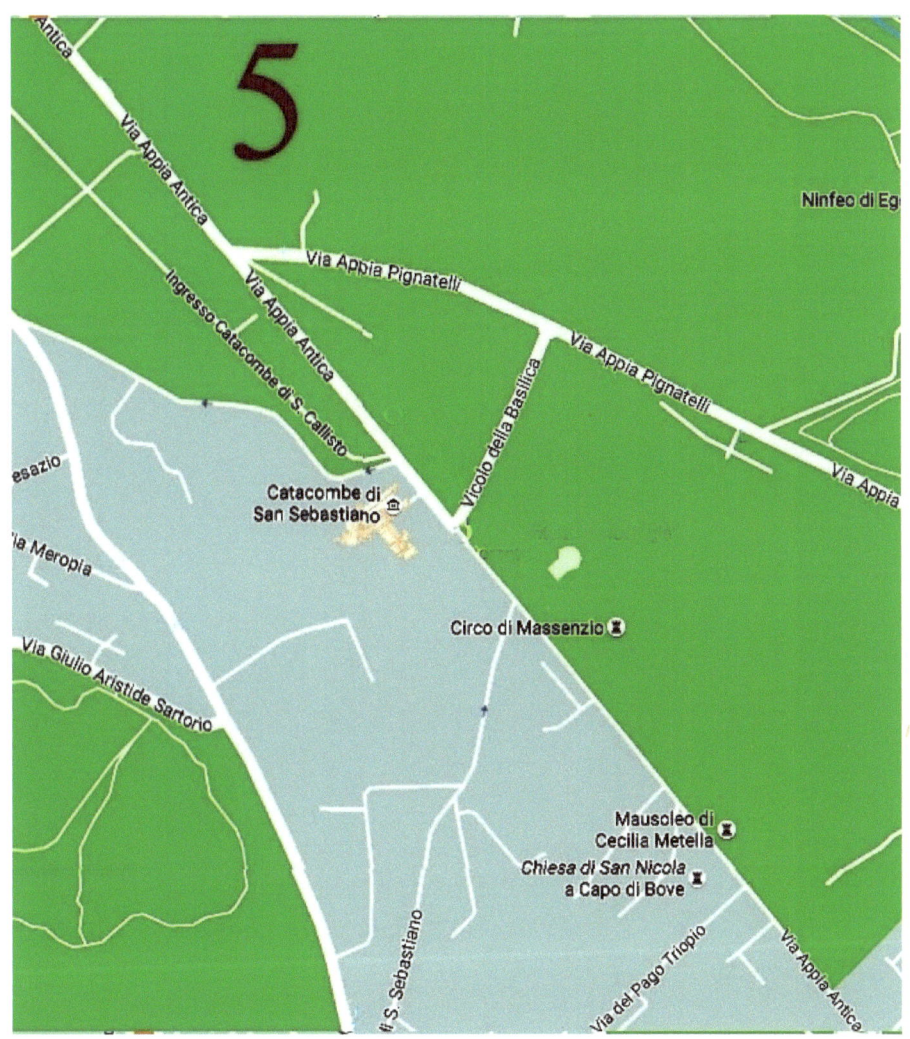

The Caffarella valley

The Caffarella valley is a large green area (19.6 km²), in the heart of the Rome city. When the Caffarelli family became owner of the area, the valley was called: Caffarella Valley. The valley is of alluvial origin and was created by Almone river, that still flows there. The river has dug the tuff deposits that have been formed as a result of eruptive activity of the Alban Hills. Nowadays you can still see the walls of tuff that dominate the bottom of the valley, formed by the alluvial deposits.

Currently the valley is part of the Appia Antica Regional Park. The valley, over the centuries, has been the subject of legends because of the presence Almone River, which was sacred to the ancient Romans. There are still traces of the sacred wood dedicate to the Romans and visible remnants of the Nymphaeum of Egeria. In this place, in ancient times, it was believed that Numa Pompilius met the Goddess Egeria, because it was believed his wife and adviser to the king.

A look at the nature of the valley

The valley, since ancient times, has been flourishing because there was always abundant of water in the area.

Woods, meadows, wetlands, vegetation, have always made it an unique and particular area, but now, after all human interventions to take advantage of this great resource, the naturalistic structure is changed.

But all is not lost; if human intervention changed the natural history of the area, on the other hand, has often allowed the development of favorable structures.

So near to small woods with old trees, there are those developed because to the recent human intervention.

There are countless animal species that thrive in this rich environment of plant, species and water.

A dedicated book needs to speak broadly of all; so here only plants and animals species, that can be encountered during a walk in the valley, are described.

Birdwatchers and nature photographers, certainly, are attracted by the possibilities offered by Caffarella Valley.

Mammals: Savi's vole, wild rabbit, Crocidura, weasel, marten, hedgehog, shrew, dwarf bat, black rat, Horseshoe Bat, curly, brown rat, mole, rat, wild mouse, mouse-eared fox.

Birds: owl, bird, gray heron, scops owl, martins, barn owl, snipe, reed warbler, reed warbler, blackcap, crested lark, goldfinch, blue tit, great tit, owl, hooded crow, cuckoo, common gull, herring gull, moorhen, kestrel , kingfishers, black kites, blackbird, sparrow, lapwing, robin, pigeon, woodpecker, buzzard, swallow, swift, wren, warbler, starling, bunting, jackdaw, stiff neck, turtle dove, corn buntings, hoopoe, nightingale greenfinch, serin.

Amphibians: green frog, tree frog, common toad, green toad, salamander yellow and black, vulgar newt, crested newt.

Reptiles: rat snake, four-lined snake, gecko, emidattilo, lizard, grass snake, lizard, slow worm, Aesculapian snake, turtle, viper

Flora: maple, buckthorn, reeds, oak, dogwood, horsetail, English oak, gigaro, broom, oak, elm, periwinkle, oak, white willow.

The birth in the Caffarella Valley

The Egeria nymph

The nymph Egeria is of the second century, as evidenced by the materials used in the bricks that compose it. On the back, the water flows from a statue of the God Almone which currently appears beheaded.

Legend says that Egeria was the lover and adviser of King Numa Pompilius. On his death, the Goddess broke into tears generating a source of water.

Egeria was one of Camene nymphs and therefore the valley source was called Vallis Camenarum.

In the second century Herodes Atticus converted the natural cave in an enclosed structure. The structure was covered by vaults of the apse type. Inside it was placed a statue of the goddess Egeria was placed. The walls were covered with white and green marble, the floor was adorned with green porphyry mosaics.

The Almone river

The Almone river originates from Colli Albani and then throws into the Tiber river. Currently, the river is called Marrana Caffarella from the Roman.

The Romans identify this river with the God Almone, who was able to give both water or drought.

Almone was the son of shepherd Tirro, who took care of the royal stables of the Latin King. Almone was succeeded to tame a deer, but he was killed by Ascanio (son of Aeneas). The fact triggered a brawl between the Trojans and the Italic shepherds. During this fight, Almone was killed. At last, Almone was deified and the river became the incarnation of the God.

The river, in the period of ancient Rome, it was the scene of ceremonies in honor of the goddess Cybele. The ceremony was performed on March 27 and was called Lavatio Matris Deum. Every year, the black stone was carried in procession and washed in the water of the river along with the sacrificial knives.

The Vaccareccia farmhouse

In 1529, the Caffarelli family began to unite various plots of land in a single estate. At the center of the estate it was built the house. During construction, a twelfth-century tower, made of blocks of tufa and marble chips was incorporated. The porch of the house has granite columns with capitals and the main floor was the first floor.

Currently, the house is home to a farm, but its status is almost abandoned. On 2012 a restoration of the structure performed.

To access the area, where there is the house of Vaccareccia, it is necessary reach the entrance of Via C. De Bildt located near Largo Tacchi Ventura. Following the directives to Tacchi Ventura, you ask for right direction. Or entering from Tacchi Ventura, once you get off in the valley, you can take the right path and take a walk, not long, until you reach the house.

The tanker called "Barn of Torlonia"

The cistern called the Torlonia barn has a rectangular shape. Dating back to Rome emperor. It has dimension of 14.5 X 5.5 meters approximately. On2011, part of tank collapsed.

The Columbarium of Constantine

The Columbarium of Constantine is a small temple dating from the second century. The size of the base is 5.4 X 7.8 meters approximately. The state of preservation is good up to the roof, that was probably the type with two slopes. Its use as a mill lasts until the Middle Ages. Between the seventeenth and the eighteenth century, a fire destroyed it, decreeing the abandonment.

On the ground floor there was the burial chamber. On the walls of the room there were niches containing the ashes of the dead. In front of the main entrance there were two columns that don't exist nowadays. Probably, rituals and celebrations in honor of the deceaseds were held on upper floors.

Roman cistern

The Roman cistern was built on two levels and it dates back to the early era of imperial Rome. Probably originally it was a burial place and then it was used to collect rainwater.

The **Valca Tower**

Valca Tower dates back to the twelfth century when the Counts Tuscolani fortified the Caffarella area. The tower was built with blocks of tufa, lava stone and marble. It had a drawbridge connected to the first floor. The people crossed the river Almone near the tower by a small wooden bridge. The tower owes its name to the fact that, being rich of water, offered facilities for washing and processing of woolen cloths (called Valche, a term derived from Longobard walkan).

The Tomb of Annia Regilla or Temple of God Redicolo

The current name was given in the nineteenth century, but it doesn't defines the funerary complex exactly. To understand it is necessary to know something of the life of Annia Regilla. Appia Annia Regilla Atilia Caucidia Tertulla was a member of a Roman noble family. When she was fourteen, she married Herod Atticus who was forty years old. Herod was a political man, angry and violent, that taught rhetoric. The man was socially important because, among its students, there were two future emperors. Because Herod was of Greek origin, after a short period in Rome, moved to Marathon in Greece with his wife.

In Greece, Annia Regilla become priestess of the goddess Demeter and the goddess Tyche. Demeter (equivalent to the Roman goddess Ceres) was the goddess of the family violence victims, the environment, the harvest and the marriage.

Instead Tyche was the goddess of fortune.

Annia gave birth to five children, and when she was pregnant with her sixth child, was killed by Alcimedonte who beated her to death.

Annia's brother accused Herod because he thought that he was responsible for the murder. But Herod was a friend of the emperor, and he was acquitted. Herod feigned a great sorrow for the death of his wife, and asked a poet to write a panegyric dedicated to his wife. The eulogy was engraved on two strains.

The stones have come down to us because they were found in front of the church of San Sebastiano. At present the memorial stones are in the Louvre Museum.

Annia Regilla was buried in Greece, but we do not know exactly where. Meanwhile Herod takes possession of the property of the Annia Regilla family. Herod called the property Triopio.

In Triopio, Herod built in memory of his wife, a cenotaph and a temple dedicated to Ceres and Faustina.

In the eighteenth century, the temple was used as a barn. A farmhouse (still visible today) and a tower belonging to the defensive system of the valley are of the same period.

The temple is spread over two floors and sits on a podium.

The material used is a yellow brick, while the decorations are cooked yellow. The lower floor was located the death chamber. The ceremonies in honor of the deceaseds took place on the first floor. In front of the façade (eastbound) there was a portico with four columns which allowed access to the upper floor. Instead the wall southbound had two semi-columns with Corinthian capitals embedded into the wall.

Temple of Ceres and Faustina

The temple is in a dominant position over the valley. The name of St. Urban was given in the ninth century in honor of the martyr bishop at the time of Marcus Aurelius.

In fact, the temple was used in the ninth century by Basilian monks who transformed it into a Christian oratory. The monks dedicated the temple to St. Urban and today the place is also known as "the Church of the Santo Urbano Caffarella".

The temple is prostyle type and is placed on a podium with a ladder with seven steps. The structure is made of brick and the decorations were made with marble from the quarries of Herod Atticus in Greece.

Internally, you can see the coffered vault with stucco which represents the apotheosis of Anna Regilla.

On the walls there are pictorial representations dating back to the tenth century.

The current appearance comes from the activity of Pope Urban VIII, carried out in 1634, who added a brick wall between the columns of the front portico.

Visit the temple during this period is difficult because access is not free; it is therefore necessary for a visit to ask for an appointment.

Equipped areas

Many of the valley areas are equipped adequately to allow picnics, sports and recreational activities. There are tools for gymnastics, playgrounds for children, benches on which to rest and admire the gorgeous scenery, the typical small fountains of Rome (called "nasoni" meaning big nose) to quench the thirst.

Many gyms carry athletes to train outdoors.

Many people do, usually jogging or cycling along the paths of the valley.

No one would have thought that was possible: in the heart of a city like Rome an area, where there is the opportunity to get closer to nature, to know, to learn to love it.

Walking along the paths

il gallinaio

Other books of the series Live in Rome

Villa dei Quintili

The new book by Stefano Benedetti Villa dei Quintili adopts the proven formula: photographs (to allow a visit to those who can not travel to the site in person) + text (to tell everything I know on this site). The book inaugurates the necklace Live in Rome, a series of easy books that reveal the places of Rome less known and more interesting. The archaeological area of Villa dei Quintili is certainly a place that can not be ignored, both for its size and for the wealth of exhibits. The book also provides detailed guidance on how to reach the site by public transport and other useful information.

Tiber Island

The fourth book in the series Live Rome dedicated to Tiber Island. The island is in the middle of the Tiber River in the stretch where the river flows in the heart of ancient Rome. The island is rich in history as evidence of its presence over the centuries. The book is a detailed guide to the discovery of this vast cultural heritage. The book is full of photographs that allow a virtual tour to those who can not go to Rome. The book also provides detailed information on how to reach the island from different parts of the city by using public transport. Additional facilities include several maps.

BOOK TOPICS:

HOW TO REACH THE TIBER ISLAND
THE LEGENDS ABOUT ITS ORIGIN
HISTORY
THE CAETANI TOWER
FABRICIO BRIDGE AND CESTIO BRIDGE
THE BROKEN BRIDGE
THE TIBER PORT
THE OBELISK
JACOMETTI NEWSSTAND
THE CHURCH OF SAN BARTOLOMEW
TEMPLES OF FAUNUS AND VEIOVE
FATEBENEFRATELLI HOSPITAL
ORATORY OF THE "RED LARGE SHIRTS"
ISRAELITE HOSPITAL
CHURCH OF ST. JOHN CALABITA
THE FLOOD OF THE TIBER AND THE TIBER ISLAND
FAUNA AND FLORA
TEVERE EXPO
PLACES TO VISIT NEAR THE TIBER ISLAND

Other books published by the author

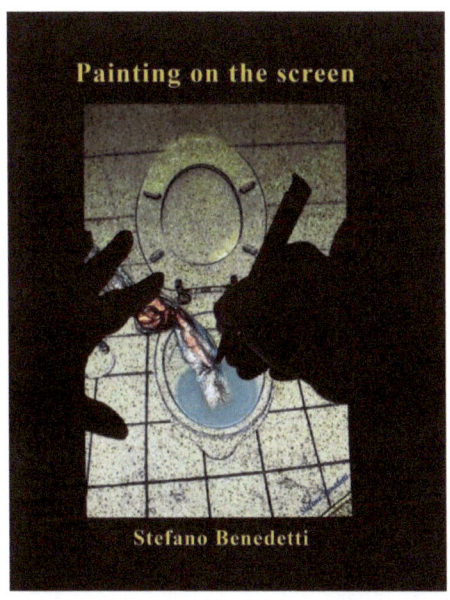

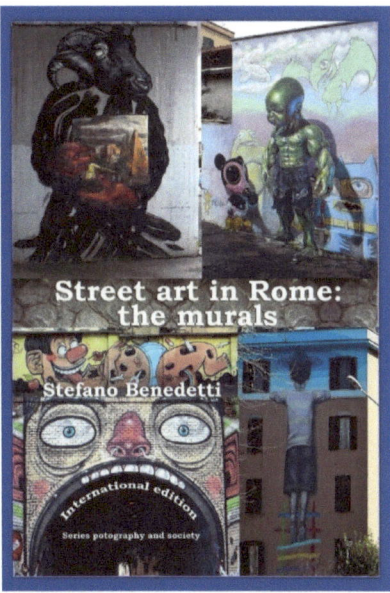

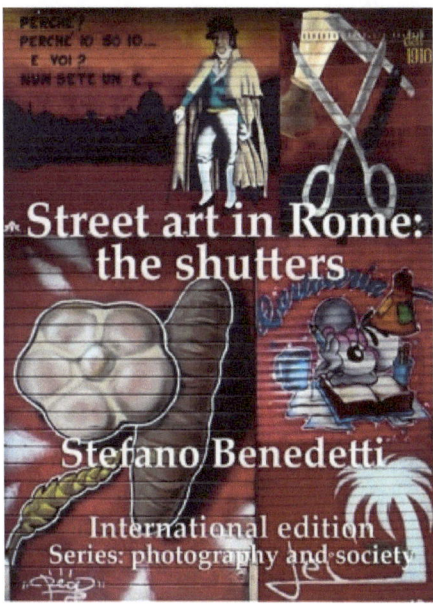

Cameras estimates
1900-2000

Stefano Benedetti

English edition

Series: Photography and society

Camera lenses estimates
Stefano Benedetti

International edition
Series photography and society

Fotografia:
la storia dell'arte e dell'ingegno

Stefano Benedetti
Collana Fotografia e società

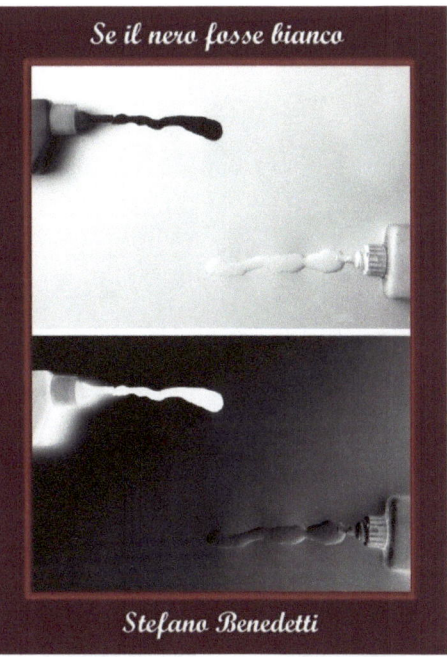

Se il nero fosse bianco

Stefano Benedetti

Fiabe per adulti
Stefano Benedetti
Seconda edizione

Fiabe dell'amore e del piacere
Stefano Benedetti Seconda edizione

Antalogia
Volume I: le finestre
Stefano Benedetti

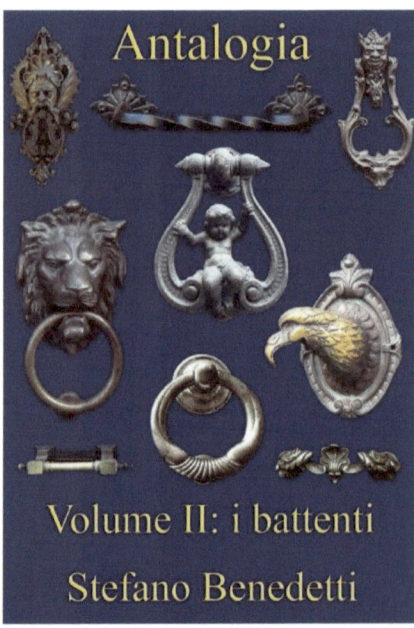

Antalogia

Volume II: i battenti

Stefano Benedetti

Antalogia Volume III: i portoni
Stefano Benedetti

Noi, quelli di città
Stefano Benedetti

Allium, cioè proprietà farmacologiche, storia, coltivazione, ricette e benefici dell'aglio

Stefano Benedetti

Collana: Alimentazione e benessere

Allium Cepa

cioè tutto quello che è utile sapere sulla cipolla

Stefano Benedetti

Collana: Alimentazione e benessere

Juglans Regia, cioè la ghianda di Giove più importante: la noce

Stefano Benedetti

Collana Alimentazione e benessere

Malus domestica, cioè il pomo della conoscenza: la mela

Stefano Benedetti

Collana Alimentazione e benessere

KRENF

STEFANO BENEDETTI

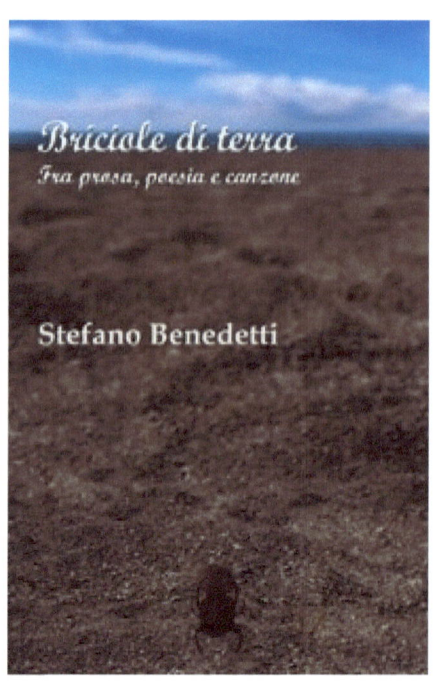

Briciole di terra
Fra prosa, poesia e canzone

Stefano Benedetti

Poesie proibite

Stefano Benedetti

Fotografia caleidoscopica

Stefano Benedetti

Collana Fotografia e società

Ritratti
poesie matematiche
Stefano Benedetti

Il magico numero nove
e i suoi amici multipli

Stefano Benedetti

Le quotazioni di 2200
apparecchi fotografici
dal 1900 al 2000

Stefano Benedetti

Collana Fotografia e società

Le stime degli obiettivi fotografici

Stefano Benedetti

Collana fotografia e società

Book distribution

The books in ebook and hard copy are distributed worldwide from Amazon and Createspace.

Many are also distributed by Kobo, Ilmiolibro, IBS and many other national and international stores.

www.ingramcontent.com/pod-product-compliance
Lightning Source LLC
Chambersburg PA
CBHW040310010626
45792CB00022B/99